21 Ways Miss You

Rachel Read

BookLeaf
Publishing

21 Ways to say I Miss You © 2022 Rachel
Read

Presentation by *BookLeaf Publishing*

Web: www.bookleafpub.com

E-mail: info@bookleafpub.com

ISBN: 9789357691635

First edition 2022

DEDICATION

To all the people I've ever missed.

Especially the ones who stayed as long as they could.

ACKNOWLEDGEMENT

Thanks to all the people who have read and liked and encouraged and appreciated any poems I have written so far. I hope they helped.

17.10.2017

Some people have it worse than me,
Maybe they're a Syrian refugee,
But it doesn't feel like that today

Some people have it worse than me.
We had 26 years, perhaps they only had three,
But it doesn't feel like that today

Some people have it worse than me
They don't have Dads or siblings or an aunty
Or best friends and family friends, you gave us
so many
But it doesn't feel like that today

Some people have it worse than me
But most people have it better
Most people aren't missing their Mum constantly
That's what I'm feeling today

17/10/17 The worst day of my life

She Showed Us The Way

She showed me the way.
So now, how do I find the way
Did she show me enough?
Do I remember what I know?
I do not have to do it alone

She showed me the way to know;
To learn more, to think, to grow.
She showed me the way to help;
to share, to love, to give: to all.

She showed me the way to make;
Make friends, make memories.
She showed me the way to hold on;
to the good ones. the ones that support,
the ones who are the best at their things,
The ones who have stopped me falling too far,
who have pulled me back up, who have lived for
me.

She showed us the way to be strong;
stronger together, protect each other,
be everything and anything we could be.

She showed me the way to laugh;
to live well: laugh often and love much

We'll Get Through It Together

Bad things have happened
But I'm doing fine
It's possible to survive
You do yours, and me mine

I don't have to help others
No one's forced to
But everyone needs someone
And maybe it's me that's for you

There's some people I meet
I can sense something amiss
They've got the discrepancy
Between something gone and here; this

It could hurt me too
To share in their pain
It can feel irretrievably much;
The sun snuffed by the rain

So I can't always be helpful
Not when I'm at my worst
That's when they're there for me
Support eases the curse

And when I'm OK
Or even fine, often good
Then support is my support
I'd do anything if I could

To help you out of sorrow
Or struggle, or the dark
By chatting or tea or
Whatever hits your mark

I only can try
And sometimes I'll fail
I'll be sad when you're sad
Though Time may heal, she's a snail

Then I'll smile when you smile
And we'll laugh through it all
When it just feels like downs
We'll find the up albeit small

Because love and laughter
Are all that I need
If we hold on to them tight
We'll be sure to succeed

1st March 2019

500 Days sounds like so many days
Working out how to live without you
But sometimes it feels like no time at all;
This me is still brand new

500 Days falls on this significant date
When you went into labour and I made you wait
Because exactly midnight is when I wanted to be
born
28 years ago

So my birthday is tomorrow
And older I'll be
There'll be at least 500 more steps
On this emotional journey

There's been highs and lows
And there'll of course be more
I know that you're still guiding
Of that I'm sure

Grief is just love with nowhere to go,
Love and grief entirely intertwined.
But I'll risk grief for the love, I'll never stop with
the love,
And like you I'll try to always be kind

It's hard to write a funny poem

It's hard to write a funny poem
When all your thoughts are sad
I do not want to write something
That will make people feel bad

Why can't all people just be kind
Be less selfish, listen, and share
Only after helping others should
We think about self-care

I want joy after the revolution
So we need it on the way.
We all have the power to change the world
With what we think and do and say

Is it possible to change the world
With a smile, a dance, a song?
Or maybe the things that make us laugh?
Whatever. Together we can't go wrong.

I Think These People are my Friends

The person who replied to my message
The person who asked if I was ok
The person who went for a walk with me
The person who already knew what I would say

The person who made me laugh
The person who bought me tea
The person who I chatted with for hours
The person who reminded me to breathe

The person who stayed as long as they could
The person who gave me jam
The person who I tried to support
The person who helped me to plan

The person who trusted me with their secrets
The person who told me their woes
The person who shared their joy with me
The person who sent handwritten notes

The person I felt safe to say weird stuff to
The person who played an online game
These people made me feel less lonely
I hope I helped them feel the same

Grieving the Life not Lived

The internet does not agree
whether you were stillborn
Or I miscarried
All that's certain is you were here

They said we did nothing wrong
There was no way to change the path
I wish I could give you life in a song
Because I know for sure you were here

Each day there is a new dawn
It will seem to some like nothing changed
Perhaps not stillborn but still born
I will never forget you were here

The loss is yours more than mine though
You died before you could live
Your age was less than zero
But it will forever be true you were here

The Agony of Being Ordinary

There's an argument happening most of the time
In the room inside my head
I could ignore them and pretend I'm fine
Or listen to what's being said

There's the voice that says I'm not good enough
Look at all the ways you could be better?
There are people getting awards for their stuff
Is it because you don't do things to the letter?

Then another agrees yes we're terrible
We're barely scraping by
You're only successful because of bias
Or because they're being kind

It's because the system is broken!!
A frustrated one loves to shout
It's people who fit in the box it works for
We're the best, there's zero doubt

A quiet one pipes up then
But it works for a big majority
It might not be that it is broken
Just that we're extraordinary

Just a bit too special I guess
one of the shrill ones sings
Not normal enough to be ordinary
But not outstanding at normal things

Think of the bigger picture!
The others all frown as this drops
Compared to the rest of the world
Even the worst of our colleagues are top

That does not make us feel better
We know others have it worse
But even stupid feelings are valid
It's tiring to live with curse

I'm not sure there is a solution
Except to choose my own way
It's agony being ordinary
But it's worse not being me any day

I have been lucky and unlucky
I am mostly free to be unique
The same as everyone else
All being different shouldn't be bleak

All being different is the actual dream
Some way to celebrate that
Congratulations for standing out

The homogeneous group would fall flat

But no one's difference is better or worse
So who then gets the money
If only we could live on hugs and smiles
And that it was always sunny

Betwixmas Carol (2021)

God rest ye merry, everyone
Let nothing you dismay
Because even though seems Covid
Will never go away
At least we have each other
Friends, family, together say

O tidings of comfort and joy (comfort and joy)
O tidings of comfort and joy

God rest ye thoughts inside my head
You were exhausted earlier today
Why are we in the dark awake
When there's nothing to dismay
We've got stuff to do tomorrow
Hope the weather isn't grey

O tidings of comfort and joy (comfort and joy)
O tidings of comfort and joy

Reflecting on Lockdown(s)

Let's not forget the world's inequality
We still cannot let them win
Write down everything that we were fighting for
Before this massive distracting thing

In a way it's made us all come together
Every single person behind one cause
But it turns out the best solution
Is to put all group activity on pause

We'll have to stay strong some other way
It's even more important to be kind
It feels like the world is over
It feels like I only exist in my mind

But I still have everything I had before
Presuming people don't forget me
Anything I can do to help I will
Let me know what support I can be

What's For You Might Be Fleeting

"This too shall pass" is comforting
When the world is doom and gloom
But it's also true for joyful things
And I'd rather they stayed in the room

 "What's for you, won't pass you"
Is another one they like to say
Fits ok if it's an opportunity that
Will definitely come up another day

Thing is, sometimes what's for you is fleeting
It being gone doesn't make it wrong
Don't forget things for only passing
Hold them close; write them a song

Learn from the things you've had to grow from
That you've struggled to live without
They are some of the most beautiful
And that's what Life is about

TFFRR - the comic relief

One upon a time at a uni friend's show

Audience of two or three, plus me

I laughed extra loud from the front row

So they definitely knew it was funny

The next day, three of us were chatting

And we were told by the lead

That backstage the resounding feeling

was "Thank Fuck for Rachel Read"

I enjoyed that phrase a lot

And thought, what is it that I need

To do for someone to make them think

Thank Fuck for Rachel Read

Now every time I support someone

After every single good deed

There's a part of me that's hoping for

A Thank Fuck for Rachel Read

So if you're ever grateful I exist

Or want to give my ego a feed

Then I think the phrase you're looking for

Is Thank Fuck for Rachel Read

And in a hundred years or so

As well as world peace and equality

I really hope I'm remembered with a

Thank Fuck for Rachel Read

Identity

Imagine the default was both
Instead of this or that
Let me love both intensely
Arts AND science, dog AND cat

Or perhaps the default is either
I'll use whichever, go with the flow
You don't have to be sure and pick a side
Just freely hang out in I don't know

If we weren't told over and over
That it's only normal to be straight
Would you have tried different hats
Has the patriarchy chosen your fate

If the default was we all COULD like everyone
Some people would still pick a spot
It's a fluid spectrum of diverse combinations
You're either in love or you're not

Imagine the default was maybe
Maybe colleagues or Best Friends
Maybe you don't like people
Maybe love is something that bends

One size never fits all
It's maybe untrue that it even fits most
Loads of us hide, scared to be Other
Imagine the joy if the default was both

Poem lamenting but also appreciating the complexity of life

Would that it twere so simple
Or as easy as you act like it is
Oh just do that and it will be done they say
The answer is surely just this

But the situation is a lot more nuanced than that
So much is happening inside my head
I feel strongly about conflicting things
I want to be everywhere and stay in my bed

My favourite me is super supportive
Is making a difference to your day
But there's so many great yous that bring me joy
It's hard to decide how to go my own way

Would it really help if it was more simple
Perhaps not because I know that it's fun
To play in the chaos, or solve something
complex
Help me love that I've too much going on

It's Not Your Fault

My pain is not an accusation
It's an escalation
An accumulation
But it's not your fault

I know you feel a responsibility
a duty
But don't feel guilty
It's not your fault

Even though you were the trigger
That's because of me not you
The trigger was not your intention
And it makes it worse if you are blue

I'm not asking you to be different
I just need you to stay
To not dismiss my pain but help me
We can both make it a brighter day

I'm so sorry to cause you discomfort
I wish it was joy always
I want to support your every endeavour
I'm grateful for all of our days

I Was Left When You Left

I was left when you left
I know you didn't want to go
Being left behind is scary
Until I'm reminded I'm not alone

I'm different to I was 5 years ago
Although in some ways I'm the same
Circumstances have caused me to grow
But I'm still funny and loving and strange

I've made friends who have pulled me from
darkness
I've made friends who are amazing and wise
Friends I'm sad that will never meet you
And ones you met who have stayed by my side

Sometimes it feels like it's only those people
That without them I would not have survived
But actually the survival I've done myself
It's them that have helped me to thrive

The world is causing a lot of trouble
There's a thousand ways people are in pain
But I'm passionate about being supportive
And together there's a lot we can gain

What will it be like in 5 more years
Even if society is burnt to the ground
I'll be holding on tight to my favourites
Seeking the joy wanting to be found

Thanks to my family and my friends that are
family
When I'm high risk you sometimes get hurt
I'll forever be sorry and grateful
Life is so often just so much effort

I still have hope for the future
No point wishing it was simple and easy
I want to pass on what I have learnt
And laugh with the funny peculiar me

Why We Didn't Talk

It doesn't seem legit to be missing you
You're literally sitting right there
But the discrepancy I can feel
Sends me to a pit of despair

There's a thing called
Physically Present, Emotionally Absent
You do it when you're not well
Something's made you sad or worried or mad
But what, you never tell

And it's extra strange because
Before, you said everything
I knew loads of the ups and downs
But then now it's only all business
What's missing makes my heart pound

I wish there was a way I could help you
But if I mention that I'm feeling bad
You think it is your fault and it makes it worse
And both of us are even more sad

Then somehow it does get better
The thing went away or you worked it out
And suddenly you're back and it's joyful

The love replaces all the doubt

And then we talk and it's like old times
So we sit or we talk while we walk
There are things to catch up on 'cause
you were there but not there
And that's why we didn't talk

We can live like Jack and Sally if we want

If you know it, sing along

♫ Where are you? And, I'm so sorry
I cannot sleep, I cannot dream tonight
I need somebody and always ♫

You have to sing it in his strange accent

♫ Catching things and eating their insides
Like indecision to call you ♫

the way the end of the verse is interrupted

♫ Don't waste your time on me
you're already
the voice inside my 'ead ♫

The whispered two words in the background, the
true sentiment

♫ Don't waste your time on me
you're already
the voice inside my head...

[strings. drums. piano.] ♫

Squish (a platonic crush)

I want to wave and smile at you
I want to give you a warm embrace
I want to stand really close to you
I want to touch your face

But I don't want to have sex with you
That would be weird

I would like to touch your shoulder
I would like to give you lifts
I would like to live in the same place as you
I would like to buy you gifts

But I don't want to have sex with you
That would be weird

I would like to share mundane tasks with you
I want to buy you dinner
I would like to celebrate things together
I want you to feel like a winner

But I don't want to have sex with you
That would be weird

Just being near you brings me joy

I like planning stuff for us to do
I could spend all day in your presence
I want your kids to know me too

But I don't want to have sex with you
That would be weird

I miss you when I don't get to see you
I always have such a lovely time
I think you're fucking beautiful
Even a 5 minute chat is just sublime

But I can't say any of this to you
because they're the things that people say
when they want to have sex with someone
and don't think I'll want to on any day

So I constantly guess what is normal to share
To make sure we stay "just" friends
But you really are my favourite
and I hope that it never ends

There are Pieces of Me Missing

I feel like an incomplete drawing
or a statue with some parts rubbed away
like a clay pot with cracks that need filling
Lego that needs rebuilding every day

I look whole but you could put hands through
me
Frayed at the edges like an old bear
But I can be filled to the brim with joy
So most people would be unaware

There are pieces of me missing
Missing out, missing time, empty space
I have loads of great experiences
But some of the pieces you can't replace

You might think I would want to be whole again
But that is not possible here
Maybe if we went to a parallel universe
Then a whole different me would appear

I can love the me that exists now
That inside will never not miss
And people wonder what are the pieces

What is making you feel all of this

There are pieces of me missing
Those gaps represent something dear
There are pieces of me missing
That I want to always have near

There are pieces of me missing
I will always believe that is true
There are pieces of me missing
There are pieces of me missing
There are pieces of me missing

.... You

21 Ways to Say I Miss You

How have you been?
Wish you were here!
So excited that you're going!
Can we go for a beer?

It's been too long
emoji of a flame
Can I see you soon?
Does your voice still sound the same?

Let's do this more often
I had such a lovely time
Here's a book I thought you'd like
Your house or mine?

When are you back from holiday?
Are you free next Saturday?
I saw this and thought of you
I don't like it when you're away

Please may I sit next to you?
I'll be here whenever you need me
Let me know if you want to chat
I don't need you to be good company

Or I could just say I miss you
That's the feeling in my heart
and I miss you just means I love you
and always have from the very start

Milton Keynes UK
Ingram Content Group UK Ltd.
UKHW050807010724
444982UK00015B/1112